JUDY MASTRANGELO

DREAM YOUR JOY

ORACLE CARDS

REDFeather™
MIND | BODY | SPIRIT

4880 Lower Valley Road, Atglen, PA 19310

CONTENTS

Introduction 6

Using the Cards 10

Oracle Cards 11

1 Beauty 10	11 Enchanted Journey..............30
2 Birthday Goodies 12	12 Eternal Youth 32
3 Breath of Love..................14	13 Evening Star Dreams 34
4 Buttercups of Love............16	14 Fairy of the Azaleas 36
5 Butterflies........................18	15 Fairy Path 38
6 Carousel of Dreams...........20	16 Fairy-Tale King 40
7 Celestial Unicorn..............22	17 Fairy Visit 42
8 Cloud Babies 24	18 Family...............................44
9 Come Fly to the Stars........26	19 Feeling Lost 46
10 Desperation.....................28	20 Flower Child 48

21 Flower Spirits 50	40 Opportunity Comes 88
22 Forest Folk 52	41 Our Animal Friends 90
23 Frog Prince 54	42 Parade of Life 92
24 Garden Party 56	43 Peaceable Kingdom 94
25 Gentle Touch 58	44 Pegasus and the Moon 96
26 Good Luck 60	45 Protector of Nature 98
27 Good Night Sweetheart 62	46 Rain 100
28 Graceful and Strong 64	47 Rainbow Cloud Castle 102
29 Guardian of Evening 66	48 Sacred Water 104
30 Home Is Where the Heart Is .. 68	49 Sandman's Magic 106
31 Joyful Fairy 70	50 Seasons of Enchantment ... 108
32 Keep in Touch 72	51 Shy Violet 110
33 Lady of Stars 74	52 Sleeping Bunny 112
34 Light a Candle 76	53 Sweet Creatures 114
35 Loneliness 78	54 Thoughtfulness 116
36 Love of the Earth 80	55 Toy Box 118
37 Magic Happens 82	56 Tranquility 120
38 Mother Dragon 84	57 Twilight Meal 122
39 Mother Moon 86	58 Water Lily Pond 124
	59 Winter Delight 126

INTRODUCTION

A Note on Health and Well-Being

Truthfully, I am not a professional certified healthcare practitioner. I am an artistic painter of pictures, and an author. Being basically a cheerful person, I always attempt to look on the bright side. One of my favorite things is to share my artwork with others, in hopes that it will bring happiness, inspiration, and hope. Many people have said that my paintings bring them delight, as does my writing.

This oracle deck has many intentions, including sharing my artwork, along with suggestions on how to bring happiness by "dreaming Joy" in your unconscious, and attempting to manifest it to reality in one's own life. I've drawn from my own life experiences and those of others. And so I also share my thoughts about health and healing, because it is of great importance to everyone's well-being. As you know, we are all integrated in mind, body, and spirit, and good health is of prime importance. They say that "health is wealth." I'm sure a wealthy person in very poor health would give anything to change places with an impoverished person in excellent health.

Within my oracle deck I urge everyone to look deep inside to discover their innate talents that they can develop to fruition. I've drawn from my own life experiences and the expertise of others, and I give advice for simple methods of natural healing that I have done, in attempts to relieve stress and other disorders. I also give simple suggestions to improve the health of your body through movement, diet, etc. Some recommendations I discuss are to cut down on certain potentially troublesome things if they are used in excess, such as sugar, salt, caffeine, nicotine, meat, and alcoholic beverages. The reason I suggest to limit taking these things is because from my own personal experience, doing so has improved my own physical state. But I urge you to do your own research so that you may discover what are the best ways to improve your own personal fitness and well-being. Everyone is different, and we all have the wonderful opportunity to choose the lifestyle that is best for us, in order to live a long, cheerful, disease-free life.

I also encourage you to seek advice from excellent certified healthcare professionals, such as MDs or DOs, for general checkups, and for serious problems. Often it's a good idea to work along with these professional allopathic doctors, in addition to doing natural healing techniques. If you have a chronic health problem, it's advisable to find out the real underlying cause. So having an examination prescribed by a doctor for a diagnostic test, such as an x-ray, could put you in the right direction. That way you can find out the best possible course to take, in order for you to heal well.

All of these things may aid us in making the best choices so that we can become content and fulfilled, with a sound mind and body. Sending many blessings to all!

Author's Note

I would like to thank my editors, Peggy Kellar and James Young, for all of their wonderful help, advice, and encouragement in the creation of this oracle card deck. And many thanks also to Jack Chappell and Danielle Farmer for doing such a beautiful job in designing it.

To my dear and talented husband Michael, for all his love and encouragement.

Purpose of This Deck

We all have dreams and aspirations, throughout our lifetime, of doing great and wonderful things and becoming an amazing person. I'll always believe in the power of aspiring to excel to the utmost, and never giving up. I know this is often a difficult thing to do, especially in today's world of difficult times. I feel it's never too late to continue building your ideal dream.

My intent is always to spread feelings of hope and inspiration to all, by sharing my belief in the spirituality of humankind and nature. My wish is that this oracle card deck will empower those who read it to feel the great joy and love in the universe, even through the darkness that may surround us. My messages within are those of healing, of the mind, body, and spirit.

Mind Painting

I am continuing here to develop my method of "Mind Painting," which I talked about in my first oracle deck, *Inspirational Visions*. In this way I encourage you to "paint a picture in your mind" of the way you would like to be in the ideal world. I deeply feel that one can dream a vision of the joy you have always wanted throughout your lifetime. You might even have forgotten some of it or temporarily submerged it in your unconscious, because it hadn't completely manifested. Sometimes when our dreams are not fulfilled, we may become depressed and very stressed. This could be problematic because if left unchecked, it could affect our health, physically, mentally, and spiritually. I have always tried through my artwork to uplift and spread bliss everywhere. And I hope that through the use of this card deck, my sincere wishes for your joy will succeed.

About the Cards

Through the use of these cards, I share my own visions that I've painted, which I hope will be inspirational. Pay attention in my artwork to the use of colors and symbols, which are intended to impart special messages of enlightenment. Among some of my favorite symbols I use are rainbows, which have vibrant colors in the same order as the chakras. I find rainbows to be filled with promise of celebration and fulfillment of our desires and hopes. Each color has its own special meanings and healing properties, which you will feel as you become sensitive to them. Other themes in my paintings that I often use are butterflies, symbolizing transformation, and unicorns, with their feeling of magical innocence. I also have used several romantic figures from the Commedia dell'arte, such as pierrots, harlequins, and columbines. And of course I add a generous sprinkling of delightful children, fairies, fantastical imaginary beasties, sweet animals, and other creatures. They are all so near and dear to my heart.

Let yourself feel free to experience the joy to dream your life. It could be a new start for a happier, more self-fulfilled one, as I share my vision with you to look on the bright side. Each of the cards will have helpful and delightful suggestions for you to do, which could help with self-realization. Some of these are relaxing exercises, daydreams, meditations, things to envision, and even suggestions for painting pictures and writing original stories. I've also included some affirmations that can be said when you feel the need, in order to give you emotional support and encouragement. Since the study of color is a magical and sacred thing, I include comments regarding specific colors being associated with the chakras, and how concentrating on them can be very healing.

I am a lover of dance as an art form, as well as all of the other fine arts. I've studied both modern and classical ballet, as well as pantomime, and I've done a lot of dance choreography. I mention this because in some of the exercises, I've added some creative dance and pantomime ideas for self-expression, which I feel will add a touch of cheer in the experience of this deck. After you do these activities, you can be creative and develop your own original ones, of course. Have fun with this.

Using the Cards

I welcome all to enjoy this card deck, both beginners and experienced oracle card readers. Let your mind relax as well as your body, and questions you will want to ask the cards will surface.

Take some cherished time from each day to be alone in your own little world. Sit quietly, breathing slowly and deeply, as you relax and feel yourself in a peaceful state. Close your eyes or stare softly into space. Look deep inside to the mirror of yourself to see what questions you need answered, such as what is troubling you. Scatter your questions to the ether. By focusing your mind on this oracle deck, your answers may emanate from deep inside your soul, from your spirit guardians who watch over you, from Mother Nature, or from any other number of spiritual sources. Then spread all the cards lightly out on a table and pass your hands gently over them, feeling their warmth and vibrations. Next, place the cards facedown on the table, and by touching the cards your intuition will draw you to one or several at that moment. Separate them from the main deck. This one card, or group of cards, will be for your reading of the day.

ORACLE CARDS

BEAUTY
Manifest your inner soul

We all are sublime beings inside; we just have to awaken the magnificent entity within us. Have confidence and believe in your greatness. Create a "Mind Painting" image in your imagination, of yourself as a god or goddess, at the height of your development. Imagine walking, talking, and moving with poise and beauty wherever you go, like the "Graces" in the Greek myth pictured in this painting. Doing so could give you delightful feelings of youth and happiness.

Exercise

Charm and elegance are wonderful attributes to strive for. Develop excellent posture and carriage as you work at various tasks. Taking slow, deep breaths throughout the day will uplift you and make you feel rejuvenated. Do exercises such as stretches, dance, and Pilates. As you move, use your body to the utmost. If you're not used to this, don't overexert yourself. Take it nice and easy at first. Your safety is of prime importance, so if you lack balance, hold onto a support such as a sturdy counter or chair. Do a little at first, then a bit more and more as you become better and stronger.

Take good care of your body. Make sure you don't damage your skin by overexposing it to the sun. Some sunlight is good in moderation. But consider covering your skin with clothing and wearing a wide-brimmed hat and sunglasses to protect your face and eyes. Exposing your beautiful skin to the sun might result in a form of skin cancer, which could be life threatening. Use good moisturizing lotions to keep your skin soft, radiant, and looking young like these Graceful Goddesses.

2

BIRTHDAY GOODIES

Celebrate life every day

Birthdays are always full of joy and excitement. The anticipation of being with friends and family to celebrate the day of your birth into this world is a blessing. Make every day just such a celebration of your life, not only on your birthday. To be alive and be able to experience all the wonder and beauty around you will fill you with happiness and love.

Meditation

Go to a quiet room where you can daydream alone. Picture in your mind some birthday parties when you were young. Remember the warm and comforting feeling of being with people you love, opening presents, and all the goodies at the celebration. Try to recall a very special event from your childhood, and the family and friends who were with you.

You're feeling so happy that you could "burst," like the child in this picture! Try to also recollect any other delightful celebrations in your past.

Now, visualize in your mind the bright-yellow color of the third chakra. Feel this color envelop you in its happy feelings. It symbolizes playfulness, optimism, and enthusiasm. It will help you experience the freedom to be yourself. Bolster your self-esteem and willpower. With a greater sense of self, you could become more delighted with the real "you" and feel the ambition to accomplish your desires.

Affirmation

Say this when you feel the need to become happier:

"I will strive to become more creative, courageous, and full of happiness. By opening the curtains, I will welcome the yellow sunlight of this yellow chakra into my heart, along with all the other cheerful colors of the rainbow, as they fill the air around me like sparkling stars.

I will look deeply at myself today and count all the blessings I have at this stage of life. Every day is exhilarating, since I have the gift of life and can share my talents with the world. Every day will be a new birthday for me!"

BREATH OF LOVE

Share your soul with the world

Emanate the love of life throughout your being. You will feel your spirits greatly uplifted. Picture yourself to be a poetic Pierrot blowing magical heart-shaped bubbles throughout the universe, which fill the air with love.

Exercise

Sitting in a chair, or lying down, relax your whole body. Let your heavy burden of pent-up feelings of stress slowly leave you. With your eyes closed, in your mind's eye, watch stress escape in the form of vapors from your body. And thus, as you breathe out, you share your love and talents with all, with the hope that they will benefit. With each breath you take in, inhale the love of nature and the world. Continue to breathe deeply in and out, letting out, and taking in love. This can be done at any time throughout the day or evening. Remember to have good posture as you sit, in order to breathe deeply to the utmost. If possible, when you are inside for a long period of time, remember to go outside once in a while, even for a little bit. At that time, breathe out deeply, expelling the air from being inside, and then inhale the outside fresher air. You will feel your spirits soar, and your head will become more clear.

Color

Breathe deeply and slowly, in and out, and surround yourself with the healing, happy, lighthearted, and soothing soft ***pink*** of my painting. This is the color of universal love, of yourself and of others. It also represents happiness, kindness, affection, healing, sweetness, femininity, nurturing, friendship, and inner peace. You can see why it's such a popular color. It is more cheerful and softer than the similar color of red. If you want to develop any of the above characteristics, imagine your favorite shade of pink surrounding your body.

BUTTERCUPS OF LOVE
Childhood fun

There is an old-fashioned game of childhood, "Do You Like Butter?" In this game, you hold a golden buttercup beneath your chin to see if it reflects on your skin. If your skin shines yellow from the flower, it means you like butter. It is often a delight to remember our youthful games we enjoyed. Any memories of them tends to make us happy.

Relive a happy memory

Close your eyes and do a "Mind Painting" picture of yourself as a child, in a delightful place with your beloved friends. It could be a beautiful sunlit scene in springtime such as this painting. Feel the warm sun on your face, and smell the delicious grass and flowers. Pretend to drink in vibrant colors of the blossoms. They will make you feel energized and vibrant. Don't hold back on laughing, singing, and dancing with your friends. In your mind, have fun choosing young friends you shared playing with as a child. Relive your delightful fun-filled times together as you share some games. In your imagination, you can also create happy events that might not have ever taken place, but that you wished had occurred.

Picture a Yellow Buttercup in your mind

Flowers are magnificent symbols of spirituality. Imagine holding a lovely yellow buttercup, and bring it close to you. Fantasize holding it and tucking it inside your heart. The cheerful *Yellow* of this flower is of the Chakra of the Solar Plexus. It's good aspects represent self-esteem and pleasure. Think of this humble little blossom when you feel down in the dumps. If it could talk to you it would say, "Enjoy life more, my friend, and give happiness to yourself and others! Enjoy the simple pleasures. Find things to make you laugh more. I will always be with you, and bring you joy, happiness, friendship, goodwill, and new beginnings."

BUTTERFLIES
Winged Spirits of Transformation

An innocent young rabbit is surrounded by his colorful playful butterfly friends. We too have animal spirits, who are our guides and helpers. All we need to do is see them in our minds, feel their presence, and contact them. Sometimes they come to us in meditation or dreams. Pick your favorite animal, who will be your "Spirit Animal Guide." Butterflies are the symbols of renewal and rebirth, as we evolve throughout our lives. The presence here on earth of these ethereal flying creatures, is a symbol and promise that we too are always developing more and more into beautiful souls. In the same way, a butterfly starts life as a caterpillar, evolving into a chrysalis, until it magically develops into a magnificent butterfly!

Daydream
Picture yourself as a tiny caterpillar, going about your everyday business. One day you feel a strange urge to sleep. As you spin yourself into a chrysalis you lie dormant, peacefully resting. But you feel strange and secret changes happening to you. You wonder "Is it a dream?" And then one day, you emerge into a spectacular and colorful butterfly, who soars away into the bright blue sky!

Create a Dance with Soothing Music
Move as a tiny caterpillar, crawling slowly upon a leaf. As you feel sleepy, slowly, contract your body into a curled-up restful position. Metamorphosis begins to change you, as you feel tingles and ripples throughout your little body. Then slowly you emerge from your dormancy, having transformed into a majestic butterfly. As you dance to express exuberance you can feel yourself filled with ecstatic joy in your change, having transcended from such a humble state into a spiritual entity. Feel the tingles all throughout your lovely wings that have sprouted, sparkling with iridescent rainbow colors. This symbolizes your Soul transforming into a Divine being.

CAROUSEL OF DREAMS

Old fashioned visions of yesteryear bring thoughts of simpler times

Carousels are an old fashioned amusement of the past which can sometimes symbolize a bygone time, when life seemed more peaceful and happy. Of course you might say that "There never were the good old days." But let's have some fun and think about them anyway! Hop a ride on your own spirited carousel horse to take you for a merry adventure.

Daydream

Go to your special room, where there is enough space for you to move around. Then you can either sit or stand to participate in these fun-filled thoughts. Try to imagine seeing all of these vivid colorful adventures in your mind.

Now hop a ride upon your own spirited carousel stallion to take you for a merry adventure. Choose a wonderful horse to be your steed. He'll be beautifully decorated with golden tassels and flowers. Pet his flowing main and hug him as you climb aboard his back and hold onto his golden pole. Then picture a memory of your youth when you were very happy. This bygone time gave you feelings of serenity, and you didn't have any cares or troubles. Walk into your picture, and join in this delightful experience. You will appear younger at the age you remember in this event, even wearing the same clothes at that time.

As you gaze at my painting of the carousel, imagine what it was like in those days, many years ago. Choose one of the people in the picture, having fun riding the carousel, eating candy, or just enjoying the cheerful happy time of days gone by. This experience will give you a new lease on life, by going into the past and being able to compare it to the present day.

Do a drawing

Keep a "magical" sketch book to jot down little drawings of glimpses in your daydreams. They could be inscribed with colored pencils if you like. This book could be added to every day, or whenever you get an idea. Let your imagination roam freely to create images of long ago, today, or perhaps events that might occur in the future. Your book could be a form of "time travel," and through your fanciful mind, you can create amazing places and events to visit.

CELESTIAL UNICORN

Fly with a great spiritual creature soaring to the heavens

This beautiful being combines a giant Pegasus, and a Unicorn. He looks transparent and seems to be at one with the clouds and sky.

The creature I've created combines two very spiritual fantasy animals. Meditate on him, and feel the message that he wants to impart to you. Make him a spirit guide, even just for a few moments.

Meditation

Imagine a beautiful sunlit sky out in an expansive landscape. As you look up into the clouds, a celestial unicorn appears. He flies with ecstatic joy and exuberance, representing our higher self, where mind, body and spirit combine to form an amazingly harmonic being for all to admire and aspire to become. He brings great love to the planet, and reawakens our feelings of childhood wonder, which we may have forgotten. He also symbolizes purity, magic, and innocence. He will lift you from any sad feelings you may have and will impart these feelings to you to give the message of hope.

Color

Concentrate on the two main background sky colors of this painting. The first is ***Indigo***. This color represents the third eye, which is the sixth chakra, symbolizing imagination, tranquility, inner wisdom, psychic abilities, and intuition. The second is a light blue ***Turquoise*** color, which symbolizes the throat, or fifth chakra. This is about truth, tranquility, and self expression. It is the mentally relaxing color of our spirit. Seek to open your throat chakra so that you are able to communicate truth easily and clearly. Learn to look within, and to understand yourself. When you do, you will be able to open your throat chakra so that you can communicate better with others. Share your natural talents with spiritual communication, and you will feel revitalized, balanced, and fulfilled.

Let the magnificent celestial Unicorn become a part of you as a spirit guide, to help you ascend to greater heights. Permit his mystical colors of indigo and turquoise to enter your soul. They will help open your being to higher transcendental planes.

CLOUD BABIES
Children and ideas waiting to be born

Little children in the evening sky, sleep soundly on soft billowing beds of clouds. This image may have any number of meanings. It could symbolize the children that you have now, or will have in the future. They are happy with you as you gently tuck them in each night, so that they go peacefully off to dreamland in the clouds.

They could also represent your sleeping creative thoughts, awaiting your mind to choose them to be born as a creative art form. You could develop them into original expressions such as literature, painting, music, dance, etc.

Meditation

Visualize these sleeping cloud babies in your mind. Cuddle them and rock them gently, as you sing softly. This will make them smile, and you can choose some of them to carry home with you as your own. Raise your cloud children with love and care, so that their many talents can blossom to their full potential. If you would prefer to have these "cloud babies" to represent your creative artwork "mind~children," and not human children, that's a beautiful thing too. Develop them the best way you can, into wonderful art forms that you love, and share them with the world. Practice this meditation often, and discover new ways to nurture your human and/or your "artwork mind~children."

COME FLY TO THE STARS

Enter the celestial plane

Have you ever wanted to "get away from it all," and just go off on a magical journey to the stars? You can do this in your imagination.

Meditation

Stand in your quiet secret room, breathing softly and deeply. Feel your troubles drift away from you like dark bubbles rising toward the ceiling. And then they magically evaporate into the air! Poof! You will instantly feel light and pure, and your body will seem to be lifting up in the air. You are becoming an etheric being. A spiritual friend from afar comes to take you on an adventure to the stars. Floating on a cloud, you both fly out of the open window into the evening starlit sky.

When you return from the heavens, you will have much to think about and dream upon. Your mind has been expanded, having traveled to celestial planes.

Affirmation

Say this to yourself when you wish to be more uplifted:

> "I yearn for more contentment, and to seek a more spiritual existence. I will try my best to become the highest person I can be, in both mind, body, and spirit. It will take diligence and work, but I feel extremely confident that I can become the ideal, that lives deep inside my soul. Mystical friends surround me, and will help me achieve my goals. I feel very strong and happy with myself in my endeavors, because I know I am kind, and seek goodness and truth."

DESPERATION
Help is always nearby

No matter how down you get, know that there will always be a light at the end of the tunnel. You'll soon be able to pick yourself up and live happily again. It may take a while for you to bolster up enough strength to continue on. But keep trying until you succeed.

My painting illustrates the story of little Thumbelina, written by Hans Christian Andersen, as she accepts the helping hand of Mrs. Mouse. In this tale, a sweet old animal welcomes the girl into her cottage, and nurtures her back to health with tenderness. The little girl goes through many trials, but eventually, blossoms into a strong spiritual being. And so, if you strive to keep hope in your soul, it it will give you courage to overcome misfortunes in life.

Affirmation

Say these words of hope and strength to yourself often. You can also write affirmations in your own words, felt deeply in your heart. They could reflect thoughts such as these, that little Thumbelina lived by:

"I am a good, honest, and loving person, and I look for people to appreciate me for who I am. I seek people who are the same, and hope that we will love each other.

I am grateful for all the kindness I receive from others, and I always will give kindness in return."

Color Meditation

There is a lot of *__orange__* in this painting. This color is the second chakra. When there is an imbalance in your life, this color could represent frustration, dependence, and emotional isolation.

Try to turn the negative element of the color orange into its positive elements. Feel yourself surrounded by a glowing orange light, which gives you wonderful feelings of independence, youth, an adventurous spirit, creativity, and satisfaction. Pour these elements into an invisible glass. When you pretend to drink this "orange juice," in your meditation, you will be greatly invigorated, and strong once again to resolve your problems.

ENCHANTED JOURNEY
Riding Pegasus to Lands of the Impossible

This great winged horse coming to us from Greco-Roman myths, is the magical stallion who rose to heaven the moment he was born. He carries the power of lightning and thunder from Zeus and Olympus with him.

When Pegasus arrives in a card, magic is sure to appear! He will help you manifest your greatest goals that you think are beyond your reach, but really are just within your grasp. Now is the time for your childhood dreams and aspirations to come to fruition.

When you ride upon him, you will rise above all obstacles, in order to achieve your highest wishes!

Color

Concentrate on the bright **_blue_** of the sky. This is the color of the throat fifth chakra, which represents imagination, loyalty, healing, trust, and the ability to communicate. You will be able to form great communication with the wondrous flying horse, and your close friend who comes with you on your voyage of discovery.

Daydream

Go to your special room, where there is enough space for you to move around. Try to imagine in your mind, seeing vividly all of these colorful adventures. Greet Pegasus as he softly lands to take you away to the land of "Dreaming the Impossible." Hop upon his back and soar through the atmosphere! Soar high above the clouds into the upper atmosphere, and imagine meeting fantastic beings. Unleash your imagination, open up your senses, and soak in amazing sights, sounds, feelings, and ideas.

How would you like to visit any fantastic land that you've ever dreamed of? Do you want to travel to a story land that you love, such as Munchkinland in the Wizard of Oz, or NeverNeverland in the story of Peter Pan? There are so many exciting things to do and places to go! You can even make up a place all of your own invention, or visit a place that you've gone to in your past that you love very much.

When you are finished with your wonderful ride to enchantment, and return home to your room again, thank your beautiful Pegasus friend for being your guide. He will nuzzle you, and perhaps ask for a hug and a sugar cube. As you wave goodbye, and he prances away, remember you can wish for him to come back at any time.

ETERNAL YOUTH

Imagination and love keeps you young in mind and body

Who would not want to visit a perfect land where children peacefully play together in daffodil hillsides lined with cherry trees? Pure white graceful unicorns join them in their daylight games. Creating scenes like this is a wonderful way to preserve feelings of youth. It seems like a perfect Garden of Eden.

Color

Envelop yourself in the varieties of rich **_green_** colors in the foliage background. This color is the fourth chakra that governs the heart. It symbolizes love, healing, compassion, harmony, and generosity.

Daydream

Be like one of the children in this painting, peacefully talking together, sharing friendship, and communing with beautiful nature. They are friends with fanciful unicorns who are as innocent and pure as they are. Breath in and out slowly and deeply. Inhale the sweet scents of spring flowers, and blossoming cherry trees. Be friends with the gentle breeze that kisses your cheeks. Remain a child in the paradise for a while. When you have finished with your peaceful reverie, and then return to yourself in present day, be sure to bring back beautiful memories of your visit to the land of eternal youth. Keep these memories alive in your soul, and you will always be young at heart.

Remembering your adventure

Here is a way that you can bring to mind again your wonderful adventure in the land beyond: Write about it. Keep a "Daydream diary" where you can elaborate on your travels through fantasy worlds. These writings can be developed into entire stories which will bring back many delightful thoughts. They will most certainly be exciting reading for others also, and could even develop into books for all to enjoy. Share your imagination!

EVENING STAR DREAMS
Live a Childhood Fantasy

No matter how old you are, it is always a delight to imagine an enchanted world. It will keep you feeling young at heart, no matter what your age. Young children live in a world of fantasy unto themselves. They feel close to animals, nature, and imaginary beings. They sometimes talk to all of them. Here are some suggestions on creating such a world for yourself.

Color
First, concentrate on the ***soft blue*** color of the sky in this painting. It is the fifth chakra located in the throat, representing calmness, self expression, and the ability to communicate clearly.

Daydream
Begin your reverie by sitting in a quite room, where you can be alone for a while. Walk into a fantasy world enveloped by this celestial blue-colored evening sky, with sparkling stars. It is a healing world of delight to create such a land of magical escape from the mundane everyday world. After you see this lovely blue color background, begin to set your stage of magical fantasy. In my painting you see the imaginary world of a child. It could be one that little ones see as a dream, or a fantasy land that they have created in their minds. I've added some sweet little animals that are children's friends. Youngsters can talk to them and share their secret dreams and wishes, in a playful way that a little person knows so well. As adults we may have forgotten how to "play." But that wonderful feeling is still within our hearts, and can be revived. You can do the same, by "Mind Painting" your own original and private world of enchantment. You can paint yourself into it, as the toddler you once were. It will make you feel young again. You can be in any place you want to be, and interact with any number of fantastic and exciting creatures. Stay in this realm as long as you wish. It will be a very fulfilling, healing, and cheering experience I'm sure!

FAIRY OF THE AZALEAS

Being Little can be a Big Thing

A little Azalea Fairy felt sad one day, and said to her mother, "I wish I wasn't such a tiny fairy. I want to be big like a giant, and stand atop a mountain, so I can see way far away. I could run and jump so high that I could touch the sun, and run to the edge of the earth in one minute!" Her mother fairy laughed, as she stroked her little fairy's head. "Don't you think that you can do many things that the huge giant can't do?" she asked. "Why you can hop around with your tiny grasshopper friends, drink delicious flower nectar with the tiny butterflies, and hear the funny buzzing stories told by the bees. That's something that the big Giants could never hope to do, because their too giant!" Then little Azalea Fairy smiled happily, knowing that she enjoyed being little, as much as the giants had fun being large. "I can sit upon my very own mountain. It's a mountain of azalea flowers!" she giggled.

Affirmation

Say this to yourself when you have the need:

> "I will remember that we all have our talents and wonderful lives to lead. We can be happy also if we strive to improve ourselves, as we see the wonders of others. But I will never forget that we too are unique in ourselves. So I will try to be of the mind of a tiny being like a Fairy, who can enjoy the intricate world of the small world. And I will also take in the world of a Giant who can experience the world of a larger view, from a mountain top."

FAIRY PATH
Embrace Life to its fullest

If you ever have a question about which way to go in life, consider choosing the way which will bring you the most happiness and love. So follow the Fairy Path, and you will find wonderful spirits who are full of Love, and will guide you on your way. Their whole existence is to express the Joy and Happiness they feel in life. They often freely share their tender kisses with the enchanted folk who live in Fairyland. But their affection never stops there. They feel love deeply for all of Nature in their magical world. And they enjoy giving heartfelt kisses of thanks to all the Spirits of Nature, such as the lovely Flowers, and Trees, Mountains, Clouds, the Sun and, the Moon. All of these entities are their beloved friends. And of course humans are a very important part of their world.

Paint a picture in your mind

Imagine these delicate Spirits visiting their nature friends. They dance with the dryad nymphs of trees, and hug them often. They fly with sylphs of the air, and swim with the naiad water nymphs of rivers and lakes, and the oceanids of the seas. And often, unseen, they flit around us humans, bringing cheer and comfort. Try to feel their presence, and picture them in your imagination. You might feel a soft kiss upon your cheek, given to you by a little Elf or Fairy that loves you. Have fun drawing images on paper that might come to you in your mind. And always remember to search for the Fairy Path! When you find it, follow that road to happiness and self fulfillment.

FAIRY-TALE KING

Have a smile and a laugh

You can't be sad and gloomy all the time! They say that laughter is the best medicine! It will certain uplift your spirits! Watch a comedy movie, read a funny book, listen to some jokes. Anything that tickles your funny bone will make you feel better! Go back in time to reread childhood nursery rhymes, such as the old English nursery rhyme "Sing a Song of Sixpence." Although it might seem nonsensical, it could really give you a chuckle.

Exercise

Try your hand at drawing funny cartoons. You could copy some drawings that you like a lot, including the funny-looking king in this picture. Start off by lightly drawing a face with just circles. Then make it into any kind of comical character that you like. If you enjoy doing this, practice drawing often. You will find it very creative, relaxing, and fun to do.

Affirmation

When you feel dejected, encourage yourself to look on the brighter side of life by saying the following:

> "I will try to keep my sense of humor, even in times of grief. I know I will try to look at things realistically to see how I can improve my life from despair. I won't wallow in dark depression and self pity. I'll try to look for the sunny side, and the "castle in the sky," which will make me smile and brighten my day. This will give me strength to carry on with my life."

17

FAIRY VISIT
Time of enchantment with the spirits

Fairies will visit you someday, telling you secrets of their magical world, especially if you believe in them. You can find the secret places where they play, if you have a pure heart, and are willing to search for them. If you feel sad or lonely, they will most certainly cheer you with their delightful stories and sparkling laughter. Once you meet them, your life will get a special dash of pixie dust to make you smile.

Color
Dwell on the **_lavender_** color which predominates the background of this picture of the evening sky. I often use this color in my paintings. It has a healing, calming, and stress-reducing effect. Let it envelop your body and wrap you in its gentle cloak. This color represents the highest chakra, the crown or seventh chakra, and indicates spirituality and higher consciousness.

Daydream
Close your eyes and picture a lovely lavender twilight starry sky. Picture yourself as a young child on a fantasy adventure, looking for Fairies and other spirits. Watch the soft billowy clouds slowly change shape amongst the stars. Visualize ethereal images in this painting such as arbors of roses. If you concentrate on the slowly moving clouds, you might see some amorphous figures begin to take shape. Lovely singing and dancing fairy spirits appear, who want to befriend you. You gladly accept their kind invitation to play, and spend a delightful time listening to stories about their magical world. They invite you to to dance and sing with them in their rose garden amongst the stars.

Dance
Play some soft and dreamy music that you love, perhaps with sweet singing. Picturing the lovely fairies, be inspired to slowly and gracefully join in their dancing and singing. Visit with them for a while, to drink in their exuberance and joy that fairies feel when they express themselves this way. Feel free to dance and sing like this often, remembering your fairy visit.

You can visit an imaginary world such as this at any time, if you sincerely believe in fairies.

FAMILY

Enjoy your close time together

It's so wonderful to have a loving family. Unfortunately, not everyone does. The security of having your parents and siblings near you really helps when going through the process of growing up. Sadly, so many families drift apart as time goes by. Animals too have families, like this family of swans. The mother and father usually mate for life, and they love their little cygnet baby swans.

Daydream

Sit with your eyes closed, and breath deeply and slowly. Dream of times gone by when your parents and siblings were younger, and you all spent quality time together. Picture your favorite and memorable activities that you used to do: outings you went on, playing together, talking with each other, etc. Imagine in detail how everyone looked several years ago. Relive some memorable conversations you had with each other. They could be funny times when you laughed and chatted about cheerful things. Or there might have been serious talks, sharing deep feelings with one another.

Now have some imaginary conversations that you wish you had had with your family, but never did. This could also be very helpful and consoling to you, even if some of your family are no longer around. You can at least communicate with the memory of your family members. But try your best to be in touch with your family who are still around, as much as possible. Reconcile any differences you may have had, which might have made you more distant at this time.

Affirmation

Repeat this as a way of reaching out to family:

> "Life is short enough, not to be close with my own family. It is a warm and comforting feeling to know that they are still there for me, and I am there for them. I will always remember my dear family members who are no longer on this earthly plane. They will forever be in my heart and I won't forget them. Love is the answer."

FEELING LOST
You will find your way

Sometimes we lose our way along the path of life, and we don't know which way to go. We often experience our ups and downs, but if events really go downhill, the future might seem bleak. If the forest that we find ourselves in becomes dark and dense, we might become desperate to find our way. But never give up looking; there is always hope!

Dream Pantomime

Retreat to your quiet room away from the hustle and bustle of life, for a period of reflection. Do movements in very slow motion, and imagine being within a huge dark forest. Walk slowly and sadly, with your head bowed, and your arms swinging listlessly. At first, walk in large circles, seeming to wander endlessly throughout the room. Then your movements become more anxious as you desperately search for a way out. Your arms wave around wildly, pushing imaginary underbrush aside, as if you're looking for something. After a little while your expression slowly changes to a more positive one, as you see a small glimmer of light coming from above. It is a star of hope lighting the sky! You know you're not lost forever! You've found your way out of the endless labyrinthine forest maze. You can finally live in the light again! Feel the freedom from all this searching.

Answers

Analyze how you feel about finding your way home again, after being so lost. Meditate on your feelings, and write them down. You will discover answers to your dilemma, and how to finally resolve your desperate situation, by seeing the candle of hope.

Affirmation

"I know that I am a wonderful and worthwhile human being. I have many talents that can be nurtured. I just have to believe in myself. I know that it will take effort on my part. And I will always remember what the great inventor Thomas Edison said: "Genius is one percent inspiration and ninety-nine percent perspiration." I will work hard to achieve my dreams and goals, and I will find it all worth it. It will be a delightful journey to achieve what I love to do!"

FLOWER CHILD

Drink in Nature's beauty

Being immersed in the beauty of nature is one of the most healing experiences you can have. Just being in a small garden is a microcosm of being within nature's vast landscape. You can experience paths of life by walking along a garden path. Sitting on a garden bench and observing the flowers and inhaling their delicious scents, is like experiencing all of life as it goes by. To observe the butterflies flit to and fro from flower to flower, and watch a squirrel run by to bury a nut, is to experience heaven on earth.

Activity

Whenever you have a chance, go to a garden, or step into your own yard to visit the flowers and trees, and watch any little wildlife busying around. It will get the cobwebs out, and renew the happiness in your heart. Breath the fresh air in deeply, and enjoy the sweet scent of grass, and perfumes of the flowers. Enjoy it with your friends, or by yourself. You are never alone when you commune with nature.

Affirmation

The following are some wonderful positive thoughts that you can say to yourself when you feel the need. You can state them either when you are inside your own private sanctuary, or out in nature:

> "I love you Mother Gaia, and all your beauty. I delight in the beautiful flower spirits as they nod hello, the tree spirits reaching out to me with graceful arms and rustling leaves, and the soft slowly floating clouds in the clear blue sky. I breath deeply of your fresh clear air. I treasure your beautiful animals who are my brothers and sisters. And I cherish all of Humankind. They are my family. I feel at one with everything and everyone. I will always greet you with joy, my Earth Mother. We all come from you."

FLOWER SPIRITS
Feel the magic art of the Fae

There are living souls within the flowers, and all of life. All of Nature is alive. Trees, butterflies, and other animals, are all living, feeling beings. Life itself is truly amazing and magical, especially because it exists in the first place. Feel the presence of the spiritual entities that live within everything.

There are so many of these beings. Just to mention a few: Undines can be found in water, Sylphs are air spirits, Dryads live in trees, Gnomes live in the earth, and Dwarfs within mountains. You can find Fairies and Elves in many places throughout nature, which look just like these little cherry blossom Fairies. Some day you may come across a nature spirit, if you believe in them and look hard enough. In the meantime, why don't you try to see how it feels being one of the little people?

Dance with Music

You can move and dance as a Flower Fairy would do, all throughout their day. Play some beautiful music that you enjoy, and then begin to move. You might start off with swaying your body slowly. And then as you get the feel of it, loosen up and move more of your body gracefully, using your head, arms and hands, torso, legs and feet. Use a flowing scarf to get into the mood, swirling and twirling it around. It could resemble fairy wings.

Begin by dancing as a fairy, as she awakens from her flower bed. She would yawn and stretch, unfolding herself in graceful slow motion. A suggestion for "morning" music could be the beautiful "Morning Mood," Opus 23 from the Peer Gynt suite by Edvard Grieg. This music depicts the rising of the sun, as it breaks through the clouds, in all its glorious beauty. Creating dance movements along with music is a delightful thing to do, when you choose music that you feel expresses your feelings. It's a wonderful artistic release.

You might feel inspired to make lovely costumes depicting Flower Spirits, and to even paint a picture of the scene you want to describe, as if you are making a stage setting. Art is the perfect means of self expression, and will leave you with a beautiful feeling of fulfillment.

FOREST FOLK
Make a visit to enchantment

When you walk along a garden path, or enter into a beautiful forest or meadow, be on the lookout for the enchanted folk. You will feel them all around you, and if you're lucky, they might appear to you in your imagination, or in real life! The world is full of magic, and you can see it if you know where to look.

Daydream

Sit in a dimly lit room, and play some soft delightful music that you enjoy. Breath deeply with your eyes closed, and imagine a magical fairy-tale woods, bathed in the glowing light of twilight. This is the time of enchantment, when the Forest Folk appear. Keep the mystical forest image in your mind that you have fantasized. Then open your eyes and stand up, as you walk slowly around the room. Continue to imagine what the tiny creatures look like who dwell in this wood. They could be little fairies, elves, goblins, gnomes, centaurs, unicorns, and other fantastic creatures. Even the animals you see might be transformed into magical beings, such as a remarkable frog with wings, wearing a wizard's hat. The trees could be spirits who move their branches like arms and speak to you.

You might feel vibrations run through you like tingling sparks, in anticipation of a new adventure. As you walk along, picture yourself coming to a beautiful Fairy Door. As you turn the knob, walk inside to the special secret section of the enchanted forest. As you enter, the light will appear as if it is bathed in a mystical radiance. Everything will seem to be glowing with a shimmering golden luster. Little creatures emerge giving you welcoming greetings into their world of fantasy. They invite you to join in with their frolics and games, and listen to them tell dreamy stories. You will always remember meeting little elves, fairies, and imaginative enchanted animals. They will invite you to visit them at any time. It will be a heartwarming experience to become a part of their magical world. Developing your powers of imagination is an exhilarating experience that will always leave you excited and delighted.

Keep an "Enchanted Forest" diary where you can jot down impressions and experiences you've had in the magical places you've visited in your imagination. And also keep a sketchbook for drawings of the phenomenal forest and creatures you have met there. Visit this place in your imagination often if you like, by yourself, or with some friends.

FROG PRINCE

Hidden treasure

To some, a frog may be a funny, almost comical looking creature. But they have very spiritual connotations too, such as being a symbol of resurrection. That is because they are amphibians, moving from water to earth. Their life seems so magical, since they go through an amazing metamorphosis, from an egg, to a tadpole, then to a little froglet in the water, which evolves into the handsome frog that we know and love! They are an inspirational lucky symbol to us, that we too have the ability to transform into higher, more joyful and creative souls!

Of course there is the famous tale by the Brothers Grimm of "The Frog Prince." In this story, a princess meets a little frog, who wants to kiss her and to marry her, in return for retrieving her golden ball in his pond. At first she is repulsed by the frog, and refuses his advances. But we all know that he is really a handsome prince who was cursed and turned into a frog by a wicked witch. The moral of the story is that one shouldn't always judge people by the way they look on the outside, because the way they are inside is more important.

(By the way, the frog in this story changed into his handsome self after the princess agreed to kiss him at last. He had awakened her heart with love.) And so we should learn this truth: "Don't always judge a book by its cover". That's because there might be a handsome special someone or some thing, lying hidden beneath the strange exterior!

Afirmation

Say this when you feel the need:

> "I will try to always search for the truth, no matter where it is hidden. At first, it might not glitter like gold, and it may not be beautiful or sparkling. But when I find it I will know that it is genuine, sincere, and honest. Be it a person, or an idea, I will take comfort knowing that I've found the true fortune for which I've been looking. And I will feel overjoyed and safe with my genuine treasure."

24

GARDEN PARTY
In a secret garden of Childhood past

One of the most delightful things in life is to be outside in a lovely flower garden with your friends, enjoying an old-fashioned tea party with scrumptious treats. It will relieve any stress you might have from the busy modern world.

Daydream

This can be done if you can go to a small peaceful section of a garden. If you don't have a quiet place to go outside, you can picture one in your mind, as you sit silently in a room. Now relax in your pretty garden, whether it's real, or in your imagination. Let's go back in time to a bygone era, by creating a "Mind Painting" in your head. Visualize yourself as a child again, with your friends. Traditionally, little boys would wear a blue sailor suit, and girls would put on their frilly party dress. Invite your favorite little teddy bear and dolly to lunch also, and be at ease on a soft blanket. Inhale the delightful scent of sweet new mown grass, amongst tall fragrant foxglove flowers near the garden gate. It's wonderfully healthy to have a tasty picnic in a relaxed mood. Food tastes more delicious when you're not rushing to finish your meal, or hurrying because you're late for something or other.

Diet tips for health

Natural organic herbal teas are a delicious drink, such as fresh peppermint tea, with a little honey. They are a wonderful substitute for caffeine drinks. A small taste of sweets are always a welcome treat, but never overdo eating sugary desserts. Savor these delicacies. Just a nibble of them should be enough. You can develop health problems if you overdo sweets. Fresh ripe fruit is a satisfying substitute for sugary treats.

When you feel you've had enough to eat, think of other things besides your food. Don't even look at the rest of the meal on your table, no matter how delicious it may seem. Take some slow, deep breaths, day dream about something, and talk to someone at your table if you are with others.

So if you want to be fit and healthy, youthful, and full of energy, envision yourself that way in your mind. Picture a good looking person that you admire, with a wonderful physique. Strive to enhance your self image by emulating them in how they look. That way you will soon be in great shape! It will keep you healthier too, and you will feel great.

GENTLE TOUCH
Give love, warmth, and healing

Feel the sweet caring in my painting, as Harlequin and Columbine gaze lovingly into each other's eyes. A gentle touch, and a kind word and action, to someone you care for deeply will go a long way. By cultivating admiration and affection among your friends and family, you will experience warmth in return. Attempt to resolve any hurts or misunderstandings between yourself and others, even though negative feelings had occurred years ago. Don't wait until it is too late to do so.

You can provide healing to yourself and others, with just a touch, and a thought:

Exercise 1: Hold your fingertips together as you take a breath and hold it for a few seconds. Repeat this until your fingers feel a slight tingle and warmth, and your palms feel warm. Then apply your fingertips to a problem area on another person or yourself. Hold your breath as long as you can, and concentrate on healing the affected area.

Please remember that if you or the person you are giving a healing touch to experiences some discomfort, stop your therapy. Most people will benefit by it, but in some rare cases it might not be the correct plan for them.

Exercise 2: To heal other areas of the body: Lie on your back upon a mat on the floor, or your bed. Place hands by your sides, and relax, breathing slowly and deeply. Then begin by concentrating on each part of your body, starting with your feet, and working up to your head. If there is a particular problem, such as soreness, concentrate on healing that. Imagine a brilliant white or green light enveloping that area and healing it. Take your time with each section of your body.

If you are attempting to heal some pain in a specific area, try gently massaging in that place, with warm hands that you have energized as I explained in the beginning. Don't press hard. Just use soft rubbing circular movements to soften tight sore muscles. With your "gentle touch" you can help melt away feelings of anxiety. Massaging the ears, hands, and feet, as well as problem areas, is very soothing and relaxing.

But if you feel that there might be a very serious physical condition which is not getting better, do research to find an excellent medical professional to heal it. They will diagnose it with X-rays etc, and if it needs urgent attention, will recommend the next step. Many doctors are outstanding, skillful, and caring. They too have a Gentle Touch, and you will be in good hands with them.

GOOD LUCK
Rainbow Unicorn

Seeing a beautiful unicorn grazing in a flower-filled meadow, with a spiritual rainbow above in the sky, is certainly a symbol of good luck. Unicorns are special creatures symbolizing magic, fantasy, purity, and innocence. They say you have to be pure of heart in order to approach one. And if they allow you to touch their magical horn, this touch will bring you healing and good fortune. Unicorns can pass magically from one world to another, even from the earth to the sky. They will teach us how to do the same.

Daydream Meditation

Go into a private room for this activity. First concentrate on this oracle card, and then close your eyes, keeping the image in your mind. In order to be able to communicate with unicorns, you should become pure of heart. Feel yourself being filled with feelings of loving kindness. Then softly approach the beautiful unicorn as he is grazing. He will let you pet and stroke his beautiful mane, and touch his shining golden horn. As you do, breathe slowly and deeply. Concentrate on his healing powers, and you may feel warm healing vibrations, with a slight tingling sensation, envelop your body. Then with your arms, reach up high toward the sky as you are standing alongside of him and his other little animal companions, in the ethereal sunlit flower meadow. Let the beautiful colors of the rainbow flood your body with invigorating and nourishing strength and healing. This is both emotional, spiritual, and physical. Stand there for a few minutes, still reaching upwards. Then lower your arms and your head slowly, and look at your dear unicorn friend. Give him a grateful hug and a kiss farewell, and he will invite you to visit him again soon.

Sit down in a chair, reflecting on your experience. Try writing about it, and draw a picture of it also. Visit your healing unicorn and magical rainbow whenever you like.

GOOD NIGHT SWEETHEART
Tender Childhood Memories

We all have memories of when we were young, being with our dear parents. Take a step back in time to one of these cherished experiences. It could be when our mothers or fathers tucked us in bed at night, and perhaps read us a story, or sang us a lullaby. Our siblings may have shared this happy time with us. The memory could be a time when we said goodnight to our own child or children. Whatever the experience was, it was certainly a precious time in our past, which would be joyful to remember and relive in our minds.

Daydream

Sit in a quiet, softly lit room, perhaps a bedroom. Picture a "Mind Painting" in your imagination of a treasured moment in your past with your parents or children, which made you very happy. It might bring a little tear of joy to your eyes, which would give you a warm and precious feeling of love. These feelings of being loved, and giving love, are some of the most sweet and memorable ones a human being can have. Even if our dear ones are no longer with us, they will always be with us in our hearts. Relive a few of these endearing times once in a while. You can visit with your cherished ones at anytime, in real life, or in your fond memories. Of course not all of our memories are pleasant, but to dwell on unhappy past experiences all the time can be depressing. Sometimes it's wonderful to relive delightful times again.

Picture yourself as a child again, on a beautiful evening with the moon and stars peeking through the curtains of your bedroom. Let the colors of blue (expansion and healing), indigo (imagination and intuition), and violet (bliss and spirituality) surround you. Picture your beloved parent(s) tucking you in bed and whispering good night. As you close your eyes you drift off to sweet dreamland, knowing that they love you and you love them in return. You could also picture yourself as the parent tucking your own child in for the night. Experiencing these daydreams will leave you comforted and inspired.

GRACEFUL AND STRONG
Becoming your ideal

Be graceful and strong as a dancer and an athlete. Take care of yourself, both mentally and physically. Our pretty Columbine and handsome Harlequin show us ways to keep ourselves vital and feeling energetic, young, and happy.

Make Life a Dance

Whatever kind of movement you do, whether stooping to pick up something, raking leaves, or sweeping the floor, use your body to the utmost. Do stretches as much as you can, even when reaching to get something up high, or turning to see something in back of you. Doing stretches are part of preliminary warm up exercises that every dancer does before a class or performance. It is in this way that they warm up their muscles and make them supple in order to display all of their amazing dance steps. So take a cue from these talented performers, to continue stretching throughout your day. It will warm up your body and make it strong and graceful, keeping you young and fit.

Even when you are doing things at the kitchen sink, you can perform little dance steps that you may enjoy. Try prancing or waltzing as you go from room to room in your home, just to practice being sure-footed and nimble. You can use a sturdy towel rack or a chair to hold onto as a support, just as dancers use a Barre.

Always do your best when you are moving, to hold your head up high, with grace and elegance, and in a tall upright posture You will be able to breathe better, feel stronger, and appear more youthful and good looking. A dancer's life is a happy one.

GUARDIAN OF EVENING
Sleeping Star Child

We all have guardians who watch over and protect us from harm. They are there to help if we need them. And they always encourage us to help ourselves to the best of our abilities. They are there at all times, in daytime and at night. Having a restful and peaceful sleep is extremely important, and our guardians will always be present to ensure our sleep will be sound and regenerating.

Pretend to be a young child again, like in this picture. See yourself sound asleep on a cloud, in the evening starlit sky, with your guardian spirit looking over you. Attempting to sense the presence of your guardian will give you comfort and the feeling of being loved.

Evening Meditation before Sleeping

This is a meditation you can try before sleeping, in order to encourage helpful and positive spiritual dreams. Reach out to your spirit guardians and ask them to protect and care for you. The following will certainly be helpful as they watch over you in sleep:

First, breathe slowly and deeply with your eyes closed, as you relax your whole body in bed at night.

Visualization: Then choose one or more images with which to create a "Mind Painting," before you drift off to dreamland. You can also think of your own original and personal images to contemplate. Here are some suggestions:

Picture a beautiful rainbow with vibrant colors, or any other image that symbolizes fulfillment and self realization to you. It could even be a magnificent tree, with roots reaching deep into the soil, and growing upward with strong branches outstretched to the sky. In your mind's eye, make a wish on a twinkling star, or by blowing on a dandelion seed globe to scatter the sparkling seeds toward the clouds. As the twinkling starlight, or dandelion seeds dissipate into the ether, your hopes and desires will emanate to the transcendental planes above.

We often have pressing problems that need to be resolved. And dreams also may contain wonderful ideas that can be put to use in many creative ways. The trick is to try to remember these wonderful thoughts when we awake. But perhaps, even if our dreams don't come to mind consciously when we wake up, hopefully they will lie dormant and influence our creative thinking throughout our waking hours. May you have Sweet Dreams!

HOME IS WHERE THE HEART IS

Keep the love inside of you glowing

Your home is a reflection of all that you hold dear. No matter where you travel round the globe, you will always have love in your heart for your special place. As Dorothy in the Wizard of Oz said: "There's no place like home!" Where we truly live includes all the the people and things that we cherish the most. And no matter where we go worldwide, home is where we long to be.

Even if the image of our dream home is only an ideal concept in our minds, which doesn't exist in reality, it is a valuable goal toward which we can always strive. If where you live is not exactly the way you want it to be, you can always work on making it into a perfect home. Think and plan on ways that you can make it more compatible to your beautiful soul.

Life is a blessing, and you can be happy anywhere that you feel comfortable. Your home can be your favorite place that you love the most. Be contented there. Decorate it with cherished objects and artwork that you love. Talk to your flowers which grow on your window sill, or out in your garden. Make them feel at home too. They flourish when you show them tender loving care.

Enjoy Your Garden

When you grow a garden, you know how wonderful it is to plan its design, plant the flowers or vegetables, and care for them. And of course, when it is completed, there is nothing like the happiness of seeing the garden in full blossom. If you don't have an outside garden, it's always fun to grow some houseplants indoors. You can even grow flowering plants on your windowsill, like African violets which bloom in many varieties and colors. It's always good to research the best way to grow plants both inside and outside. Growing plants are like growing a family, or having a pet. They are similar to children, and some people even talk to their plants.

You will find it a wonderful experience to dig in the dirt, and feel the vibrations of growing vegetation. It is a delightful exercise, and reduces stress and depression.

JOYFUL FAIRY

Bring out your happiness

There are so many things in our lives that can make us happy. Of course it's only human to feel forlorn and sad at times. But we can build on our distress to find a way out of the mist of gloom.

The Fairy of Joy will come to cheer you and uplift your spirits, if you reach out to her. Open the window of your Soul to welcome her in. She will appear, on a breeze of fresh air, bedecked in delightful sparkling dew drops and starry flowers.

Meditation

Breath deeply, seated in a room, with your eyes closed. Feel the magnificent violet color of the crown chakra emanate from the top of your head, and radiate in the air. You will feel a lovely blissful spirituality move in waves throughout your body. It will leave you warm and relaxed, yet delightfully rejuvenated and hopeful. Know then that the Joyful Fairy has visited you, and will come again often if you wish for her.

Affirmation

Whisper this to yourself when you have the need:

"Oh Joyful Fairy, please lift me from my dejection. I feel so melancholy and alone! I need to be with you, and fly and float with you through the air. Teach me how to turn my despair into hope, and my failures into self fulfillment. Help me to smile again, laugh again, and love life again! I open the window of my soul to you. Please visit with me! Oh ~ I see you now! There you are! Thank you for coming!

I am so grateful to you! I feel Blessed."

KEEP IN TOUCH
Sending a Dove letter of Love

Reach out to your loved ones, in every way you can. Life is too short not to feel their presence. Sometimes we get so wrapped up in our own lives that we loose track of the days, and forget about family and friends. Being alone is often beneficial at times, in order to meditate and create. But being in actual contact with those you care about is also a valuable blessing. Don't wait until it's too late. Even if you can't be with someone in person, reach out by phone, email, and any number of ways that are available in this modern day and age. The possibilities are many. Even the personal touch of sending them a thoughtful gift, greeting card, or letter by mail, will be something received with gratitude, because it obviously came from your kind heart. To reestablish close relationships with your dear ones will rekindle the wonderful feelings of love in your life. Remember to also continue to make new relationships as time goes on. Others will certainly be happy to reciprocate by being in touch with you, and you will have a wonderful feeling of belonging.

Pantomime

Go to your secret room and get ready for some fun. Think of one or more people that you would like to communicate with. They may be loved ones that you haven't seen or heard from for years. They might even be long gone from this earth plane. Or they could be those with whom you are now still in communication. Whoever they are, picture them in your mind, the best way you can, standing in front of you. Now without a word, do a pantomime of creating heart valentines, which well from deep inside of your soul. Draw these expressions of your love out of your heart, which is represented by the fourth chakra of the heart. When you unblock your heart chakra, you will feel a deep connection with people, and enhance your attributes of Love, Hope, Sympathy, and Compassion.

The color pink, as well as green is associated with the heart chakra. So feel yourself surrounded be a huge pink heart which has emanated from your being deep inside. Now you can put your heart valentines into an envelope. Then reach up high to greet a Dove of peace, to be your spirit messenger and carry these heartfelt wishes to your loved ones. Waving goodby to the lovely bird, you watch him fly aloft into the clear blue sky. He soon returns with thank you valentines from your dear ones. This experience will give you satisfaction that you have communicated with those no longer with you, and the courage to keep in touch with those still here on earth.

LADY OF STARS
Our guiding light

She is our inspiration and our soul, who shows us the wonders of the universe. In the darkness of existence she shines a light to open up our minds to all the amazing awe around us.

Meet the beautiful being who lives within us. We are at one with her. Contact this divinity who is inside your soul, and you will become a beacon of light to yourself and others.

Meditation

Close your eyes and picture the beautiful **_violet color_** which is the crown seventh chakra at the top of your head. It represents bliss, spirituality, higher consciousness, and idealism. Create a "Mind Painting" of this lovely Lady of Stars, appearing on a cloud from the violet evening sky. Her body is formed of twinkling stars, and she holds a candle of truth and inspiration to show us the way to ascend to greater heights. Sit on an evening cloud with her. Be open and inquisitive as an innocent child, and learn deep meanings and truths from this goddess who you yourself are becoming. Shine brightly in the universe.

Affirmation

Say this at night before going to sleep:

> "Dear Lady of Stars, I contact you this evening, to ask you to please light your magical candle to enlighten me, and bring me sweet dreams. May they be uplifting and inspiring visions, that I will remember when I awake. I long for them to guide me throughout my daylight hours, so that I may constantly become a more spiritually, emotionally, and creatively developed person, to the best of my abilities. Thank you for your kindness dear Spirit. You are my guiding light."

LIGHT A CANDLE
Let truth shine through the darkness

We all float in a vast star filled night, sometimes looking everywhere for a sign of hope.

Daydream

Picture the soft blue sky which is in between day and twilight, when the stars begin to shine and the moon faintly glows. As we look around, becoming used to the misty light, we see a faint warm yellow light appear in the darkness. It becomes brighter and brighter, as we float over to see what is up ahead. Our curiosity is answered~it is the warm crescent moon. Standing on it is the Old Man in the Moon who lights a candle of spirituality for a young star child. We sit down softly to observe this tender scene.

Meditation

When you contemplate the moon at night, you might think of it as either a masculine god or feminine goddess. Cultures throughout the ages have chosen both. Whatever gender we choose for the moon, it certainly is a fascinating celestial body, the closest one to us. As you reflect on the moon, dream on it as you would scry a crystal ball, with the hope of detecting visions. Let it inspire you with personal guidance from your subconscious mind. Try your hand at creating a fairy tale by scrying on the moon or stars. Here is how I created a fairy-tale image in my mind by "moon gazing" at night.

I began by meditating on the luminous color **_yellow_** of the bright moon. This color is the third chakra representing purpose, joy, and optimism. Then the image on this card came to me, of three figures standing on the crescent moon: a youthful star child, a young observer, and the wise Old Man in the Moon. The old man was lighting a glowing candle of truth whose bright rays of light emanated throughout the universe of darkness.

Each being gives knowledge and truth to the others from their own perspective. The young children inspire the old man with innocence, vitality, a desire to learn, and the awe of life. The Man in the Moon gives wisdom to the youngsters, because he is eternal, and has seen many things. I was inspired to create a painting from this "Mind Painting" that came to me when I gazed on the moon.

When you have tried this meditation on your own, think about the feelings and lessons you have learned from the experience. You may want to write your own fairy tale or do a painting illustrating your visions also.

LONELINESS
Your life will improve

We have all felt alone at one time or another. Sometimes being by yourself can be very productive, when you can think about yourself and analyze your situation in life. It doesn't mean that you have to be depressed. This experience can lead to building strength and self confidence, and the ability to overcome tough situations of life. But sometimes we may find ourselves in bad circumstances, such as abandonment, and wondering where to turn next. You might feel like tiny Thumbelina, in the fairy tale by Hans Christian Andersen, when she found herself alone in the world. She had no one to help her, and winter was coming. All that the tiny girl could do was wrap herself up in a leaf, and pray she would survive to see another day.

But as we all know, this sweet and kind little person did survive, and her story had a happy ending. Her reward was that she was taken to a lovely land of fairies, where she married a handsome prince, and they lived happily ever after. I firmly believe that everyone has the potential to surmount difficulties if they are good and pure of heart. Try your best to think positively rather than negatively.

Meditation

Surround yourself with the **_colors_** of this painting: The sky is a light wintery **_blue_**. When this color of the fifth throat chakra is imbalanced, it can symbolize depression, and being withdrawn. The **_red_** color of the leaves represents the first root chakra. An imbalanced attribute of this color can depict anxiety, fear, self doubt, and self pity. Sit in a comfortable chair and relax. You are going to do a "**_contraction_**" like a dancer, forming a C shape with your upper body. Feel your shoulders slump forward and your head bend down in a posture showing sadness and defeat. Imagine that you are surrounded with the colors of **_wintery blue_**, and **_dark red_** autumn leaves, like in my painting. Then slowly, make those colors disappear in your mind, and change to a beautiful luminous bright **_green,_** which envelopes you like a giant bubble. Now you are going to do a movement of "**_expansion_**" by making your shoulders slowly uncurl, and straightening your neck and head. Take a deep breath, and feel your shoulders and head go back. Sit up straight, raise your hands and head up, and feel your spirits soar. Feel the beautiful **_green_** color of the heart chakra fill you with balance and love. After this exercise, when you meditate, wonderful and positive answers will come to you, and your spirits will improve.

LOVE OF THE EARTH

Feel close to nature

As you observe all the life on earth, whether it's the tiniest cricket, or the highest mountain, you will be inspired and amazed by the miracle of life. You will know that every little thing is precious to us, and that the very reality of life itself is magical.

The miracle of birds and bees flying, flowers blooming, and squirrels climbing trees, is quite amazing. And the fact of life itself continuing and evolving for such a long time is fantastic.

<u>Meditation</u>

As you sit on the floor, or upon a chair, close your eyes and imagine yourself in a lovely forest or garden, surrounded by beautiful animals. They are playing all around you, and doing the lovely things that animals do. Observe them in their charming ways, and feel their amazing attributes. They are all blessed creatures of our planet, and we should revere them for their astonishing qualities. Even the fact that birds can construct a nest high up in the trees, that can withstand storms, is breathtaking. Always hold respect for all of life, including humankind, deep within your being. It will give you a wonderful purpose and inspiration for living.

MAGIC HAPPENS
Enter the world of Fae

How would you like to actually become a tiny elemental? There are many little creatures you can choose from, such as a sylph of the air, a tree dryad, a mermaid or merman, a sprite or a pixie, a fairy, an elf, or a gnome. This will be a wonderfully delightful experience that you will always remember. Doing this will develop your imagination, give your life some sparkle, and uplift your spirits.

Live a fantasy

Go to your secret room where you can be for a while, in order to dream a fantasy. If you want to, bring a companion with you, and you can enjoy this fun together. Or else you can be with an imaginary friend that you conjure up in your imagination. To begin, you'll have to use some pretend magic to become one of the wee folk, since you're a human. So ask your real or imaginary friend, who is an elf, to make you tiny the way he is. He will then say a magical incantation, and a bright white star will appear from his fingertips, lighting up the room with sparkling rays and tiny twinkling lights. You'll feel yourself twirling round and round, and before you know it, you will become a tiny creature just like him! Magic has just happened, and this is only the beginning! Prepare for an amazing adventure, as you become the elemental of your choice. You could be one from a fairy tale that you've read, such as "The Little Mermaid," or Tinkerbell from the story of *Peter Pan*. You can be spontaneous with your companion, and improvise an original fairy adventure that you create together. Or you could be part of a story that you've read or seen in the movies. Reach into your imagination, and "Mind Paint" how you would look, move, and talk. You could grow wings, and have fairy butterfly feelers on your head. Flying on colorful translucent wings will be an exhilarating feeling. When your fantasy world comes to a happy ending, you will return again to the human world, and magically become large again in your human form.

Having felt what it was like to actually become one of the enchanted tiny folk, is a memorable experience. It will bring you closer to appreciating the beauty of the fairy world of fanciful happenings.

MOTHER DRAGON

Are the tasks of life getting you down?

The joys of parenthood might not always be what you envisioned they would be. Sometimes everyday things mount up so high that you finally feel at your wits end, and you might feel like throwing in your broom! But think of it this way: The gift of life is a blessing to all of us. And to have the amazing opportunity of raising a dear child is a memorable experience. Being able to be entrusted with the care of an innocent little soul is heaven sent. Understandably children have good and bad days, and they can sometimes be very trying. But they look to you for love and guidance, which you certainly know how to give.

Here are some suggestions:

Games to share

Make life a lark, brimmed full of fun-filled games. Bring the fascination and amazement of life to your children. Share your love of wonderful things with them. They will enjoy your enthusiasm of interesting topics, such as a love of nature and the fine arts. Make a garden with them in your backyard, or a windowsill garden with potted plants. Have fun together watching the flowers grow. Enjoy creating things together with them, such as making something with clay, doing a painting, making dinner, or baking a cake. Read them a story, and have them read you a story. Then act out a story together, dressing up in beautiful costumes, and performing it as a play for an audience of your friends and family. Help develop their sensitivity and compassion for animals, and preservation of the environment. Do innovative things with them, such as listening, performing, and dancing to music that you both enjoy. Take a nature walk around the neighborhood, pointing out animals you see, and telling them the names of various trees and pretty flowers. The world will open up to you as well, and both you and your children will be happier, feel closer, and be the better for it. You don't have to be a Dragon mother, just a loving caring one!

MOTHER MOON
Our celestial companion

The Moon is a great influence on our lives in more ways than one. It is a feminine symbol, but it's still common to think of the fanciful "Man in the Moon." The "Lady in the Moon" is also a magical and mysterious entity, who has associations of fertility and change. We often dream on the moon, and send deep personal wishes to her.

Moon Meditation

Look out at the evening sky and concentrate on the moon and stars, in a dreamlike state. Even if you can't see the moon, imagine that it is there. Make a heartfelt wish about your true love, throwing a kiss out to the stars. Then imagine the Mother Moon's sweet face, with silvery hair, as in my painting. She smiles and sends you spiritual blessings of wisdom, intuition, and love. When you see her, imagine lovely fairies floating and dancing all around her. Watch them as they gracefully move throughout the sky, delighting the nearby stars. After a while, take a deep breath, stretch and yawn, and lie down with your eyes closed. Then create a moving "Mind Painting" of your celestial vision that you have just seen. It will be very relaxing and uplifting. When you wake up the next morning, you will feel rejuvenated, inspired, and energized.

Make Moon Wishes

Be a dreamer, and wish upon the Moon as well as the Stars. First make sure that your wishes have wonderful and positive intentions, and serve the higher good. Handwrite your wishes, since your personal vibrations will flow through your pen on paper better than by typing. Concentrate on the moon and write what comes to you when you see her. As you look upon the moon, your thoughts may wander, and develop into dream-like reveries. Write them down and see if any of your visions inspire you with spiritual wishes. Keep a "Moon Wish Diary" to write down your wishes and see if any of them come true.

OPPORTUNITY COMES
Magical surprises

You may sometimes feel that something is lacking in your everyday life. But you can't really understand what is missing. You only know that your world has become somewhat lackluster and unimaginative. So if an opportunity would manifest to you that seemed exciting, you might jump to the occasion. You would be excited to let it take you by the hand, and to go toward a new path, rather than having to continue along the tried and true road you have been on for a long time. Sometimes opportunities appear out of nowhere, in a very unexpected way. But if you are wise, you should always think first before you jump into a new and different situation. Consider if there might be any tangled webs you could fall into before you leap toward the new experience. Often, cultivating a keen intuition would be very helpful in making the very important decision as to whether or not to open the door to a new opportunity. Consider the many repercussions that could happen if you make the wrong choice. Investigate the qualifications of the parties who offer you an opportunity that would be very life changing. It might require you to give up some important things that you have strived to accomplish for such a long time.

But why don't we try a little bit of pretending?

Just for fun, live a Fantasy

What would you do if you had a surprise visit on your windowsill, by a magical elf who promised you an exciting adventure if you would come away with him? Would you immediately take his hand and join him in this fantastic opportunity? The answer might be <u>yes</u>, if you were an innocent child, who loved Fairy Tales, and yearned for an amazing storybook adventure! You probably would jump at the chance! Let's pretend that this is the case. So just for fun, throw caution to the winds, let your hair down, and join him in a fantasy! Imagine the fun of an adventure that you would have with this little elf or fairy, if they came to visit you! In your imagination, become a little girl or boy with no responsibility, who is able to jump onto a magic carpet ride to Fairyland. Don't forget to write, and come back to reality soon! Have fun with your dreams!

OUR ANIMAL FRIENDS
They give us guidance and protection in life

All animals are our friends, and they contribute to the beauty and wonder of our fair earth. They can bring us great happiness, and we are able to appreciate them right outside the window in our backyard, in the zoo, and on TV. It is inspiring for us to know that such amazing creatures live among us, and are our companions on this planet. We hope to protect them and keep them from harm.

We each have our own very special animal spirits guides and helpers. We need to see them in our minds, feel their presence, and come in contact with them. Sometimes they come to us in meditation or dreams, and bring us inspiring and helpful messages. Pick your favorite animal, perhaps one you have as a pet, or that you love to watch outside in the wild. You can have several throughout your lifetime.

Draw your new Animal Spirit guide

If you don't know which animal is your special spirit, start off by asking it to help you find out who and what he or she is. Then begin to lightly draw a sketch, holding your pencil very loosely. Relax and let your pencil move slowly around the paper. It may seem to be moving all by itself. This will be a form of "Automatic Drawing," or what I like to call "Mind Drawing." Let your eyes go out of focus, so you don't see what you're drawing very clearly. When you eventually have a mass of lines, focus on it, with your eyes still half closed. Breathe deeply as you concentrate on your paper, and soon you will see shapes evolving into an animal. When you do, develop these preliminary smudges into a picture of your new spirit animal guide. Then thank your animal for appearing to you in the picture.

Dance pantomime

Put on some sprightly music that you enjoy, in a room where you will have space to move around freely. An interesting musical composition which suggests a lot of animals could be "The Carnival of the Animals" by Camille Saint-Saëns. Upon listening to the music, imagine some of your favorite animals, picturing how they look and move. One by one, see yourself changing into an animal, and moving the way they do. Really feel the sense of how it would be to move like that particular animal. Imagine what it would be like to be covered in feathers, fur, scales, or even gills.

PARADE OF LIFE
Celebrate the joy of existence

When you were a child, I'm sure you enjoyed playing games outside with your friends. They could have been your childhood companions, little animal pets, or imaginary friends. Whoever they were, I'm sure it was a lot of happy fun. Let's remember some of those jolly experiences from years ago, which still lie deep within your heart. It's always an uplifting experience to relive these things. It can make us feel young again.

Daydream Pantomime

Sit in a comfortable chair and relax with your eyes closed. <u>Don't get up from your chair yet, just make motions with your hands and feet.</u> Picture yourself in a familiar place of your childhood memories. Do some pantomime motions of putting on the clothes that you dressed in then. Now pantomime opening the door and going outside to the special place where you liked to play. Meet and greet your friends, and enjoy a special playtime with them. You could play ball, sled, jump rope, climb trees, all in your mind, as you're sitting on your chair.

Exercise

Now as we all know, it's important that we get some exercise. Many of us are very sedentary in our everyday lives, with our work and our recreation. But we can run into trouble later on in life if we don't move our limbs. So even if you sit for a long time, remember to stand up every once in a while. You can walk or march in place for a little bit. Stand up and sit down several times. Walk or trot lightly around the room. Stretch your neck muscles, and let your head go around clockwise and counter-clockwise. Then do some stretching, reaching from side to side. It might feel a little sore at first, but stretching will feel very good and make the pain go away. Also make sure, when you are sitting in your chair, that you have excellent posture, pulling your shoulders back, and arching your back a little. Don't become stoop-shouldered.

Envision yourself as the little child in this picture, marching in a parade back a forth, with your imaginary friends. Lift your feet and knees up nicely, to give them strength and flexibility. Hold your head up high. You will feel young and healthy. Practice different exercises at various times throughout the day. You don't have to do it all at once. A little at a time will be a good start. Have fun playing!

PEACEABLE KINGDOM

Love on earth

Imagine all of the animal kingdom existing in peace with one another, and humans doing the same. The Lion and the Lamb in this picture symbolizes the ideal of coexistence of all. We can dream of world peace where all nations live together without war, and exist on earth with mutual self respect for every living creature. In this peaceful land, everyone would also respect the beauty of nature and see how important it is to preserve the pure quality of our magnificent earth. Keeping our precious air, water, forests, and animals safe and pure, is of utmost concern, in order for the world to survive well.

<u>Meditation</u>

Visualize our beautiful planet Earth spinning slowly in dark space. Picture a luminous ***<u>white light</u>*** enveloping the planet. The color white symbolizes purity, protection, and encouragement as well as peace and calm. Dwell on that image in your mind. Then change the color white enveloping the planet to a beautiful serene ***<u>blue</u>*** color from the 5th chakra located at the throat, denoting expansion and healing, as well as calm. Then picture a luminous ***<u>green</u>*** color from the 4th heart chakra, representing balance, love, and harmony, spreading its healing effects over the planet. Next, spread the color ***<u>violet</u>*** from the 7th crown chakra, which will disperse bliss and spirituality throughout our special earth. And finally, imagine a beautiful shimmering colorful rainbow of all the colors, to encircle and encompass our huge globe, and send out healing vibrations all through our sacred planet. Practice this meditation as often as you like, and therefore spread good rays of healing throughout our world.

44

PEGASUS AND THE MOON
The Fly-Away Horse

This is one of the illustrations I've done for the beautiful poem "The Fly-Away Horse" written by Eugene Field. I am often inspired by beautiful art forms, such as literature, music, dance, painting, and drama. It's always a treat to reach out to great artists that you admire, and to create an original work of your own, influenced by their masterpieces. I find that the fine arts are some of the highest levels of creations produced by humankind. Here is a section of this lovely poem:

"For it's only at night, when the stars twinkle bright,

that the Fly-Away Horse, with a neigh,

and a pull at his rein and a toss of his mane,

is up on his heels and away!

The moon in the sky, as he gallopeth by,

cries "Oh! What a marvelous sight!"

And the Stars in dismay hide their faces away

in the lap of old Grandmother Night."

Creating

Experience and enjoy many various works of art over a period of time. These could be your favorite stories and poems in books, movies, musical shows, operas, plays, ballets, paintings, etc. They could be creations by great artists of the past and present. Pick one of your favorites to start off with.

Now close your eyes, and create a "Mind Painting" inspired by this piece of art. You might just see various colors floating by at first. Soon, random pictures may start to appear. When you begin to control the passing images that you see with your mind's eye, the essence of your entire new work of art, in vivid color, may appear. You may hear music, see people dancing and singing, or see a finished painting or sculpture. When you open your eyes, you can begin the process of bringing your wonderful creation into being.

PROTECTOR OF NATURE
Love our planet

When you live life to the fullest, you will come to know that all creatures of nature depend on one another. We learn to coexist in peaceful harmony and help each other. Protecting our environment is so important for the preservation of all species who dwell here. If we watch over all, and become aware of our environment, we will help in our way to love our dear Mother Earth and all her children. That includes her kingdoms of animals, plants, the vast lands, and waterways.

We live in a very special planet, and are so lucky to do so.

Meditation

You can practice this either in your special private room, or outside where you can feel the breeze, and smell aromas of flowers.

Picture yourself on a mountain top overlooking a vast landscape of mountains, trees, and rivers. Below you, pass by herds of beautiful animals. Feel the deep love for all of this natural beauty which envelopes around you. Embrace all things: the magnificent sky with colorful clouds, majestic animals, and spectacular trees and waterways. This fantastic scene will be awe inspiring, and you can carry it in your heart whenever you need motivation and encouragement. Strive in your own way to keep life pure and to always be a "Protector of Nature." This will give you great joy, and you will give a gift to the earth.

RAIN
Liquid abundance

Some people get depressed on a rainy day. It is a very common thought that they feel it is a somber time, because clouds appear, and rain spoils their plans to enjoy the outdoors. But think of it this way: Rain is such a valued nurturing magical substance that is needed to grow plants and crops to eat, and form lakes and other waterways where animals can drink. We, as humans, could not live without this liquid sunshine either. If it didn't exist, our Earth would be a barren desert. Rain can represent rebirth and emotional cleansing, good fortune and abundance.

Dance Pantomime

Go to your secret room to have some quality time alone, expressing your imagination. Play some cheerful prancing music for inspiration. Picture yourself as a child, and join some imaginary friends in a fun-filled parade, such as in my picture. Your friends could be sweet little animals with clothes on, other children, or any number of fantasy creatures. Hold onto imaginary mushrooms for umbrellas, walk happily, splashing and hopping through all the rain puddles. Don't be worried that you will get wet, just have fun playing in the rain, the way a little child would want to do. Then put down your umbrella and turn your face upward to the sky. Closing your eyes, open your mouth wide to drink in the delicious rain water. It will cleanse and refresh you! Dance round and round in the rain with your friends, without your umbrellas, as you get soaking wet. It feels wonderful, since it's a warm spring day, and the water feels great! Run and jump in place to the music. Laugh and sing and dance around with your friends. Then come inside and get dried off, sitting down for some delicious drinks and snacks.

This little play time will get you out of the doldrums, and help to uplift your spirits. You will feel cleansed after drinking the pure clean rainwater, and getting all wet by by it. Invent other dance and play pantomimes like this one, and do them whenever you're in the mood.

RAINBOW CLOUD CASTLE
Good fortune lies ahead

Rainbows symbolize magical blessings, where dreams come true. They form a magnificent colorful bridge, from earth to the sky. And to see a castle in the clouds at the end of a rainbow is certainly a symbol of enchantment and happiness.

Daydream

Let's experience an adventure to just such a castle in the clouds. But first we will climb up a bridge made from a rainbow. They say that the best way to do that is to become light as air. So feel yourself becoming an ethereal being. Look at yourself in the mirror of your mind. At first you seem rather solid as you do on the earthly plane. But as you concentrate on yourself in the mirror of your soul, you become more and more transparent. You feel light as a feather, and are able to float and walk on air! Now you are ready to climb up the rainbow. As you begin walking upon it, the rainbow passes through you, and your skin begins to glow with its beautiful transparent colors. These are healing colors which pass all through your body and cleanse you. As you continue on your ascent upward, you finally arrive to the lovely fairy tale castle at the top of the rainbow cloud bridge. There you are welcomed by spiritual beings, who invite you to visit their magnificent cloud gardens and the glowing rooms of their etheric castle. Spend time there exploring this enchanting fantasy realm. It will be an unforgettable experience that you will always remember, when you get back to the earth plane.

SACRED WATER
The source of Life

Water is a pure and wonderful healing substance. It sustains all the Animals and Plants of Nature on our planet Earth. We could not survive without it. Life itself developed and emerged from the primordial waters, as is told in the creation myths. To date, we are the only planet with large bodies of water. We are very lucky to live in this beautiful world, with such a magical liquid.

Water has many healing and cleansing properties, and so it is an excellent practice to drink the cleanest, most unadulterated kind possible, free of contaminants. If you drink it by itself at room temperature, you will find it the most thirst quenching beverage around. It's also wonderful to use in other things such as coffee, tea, and when you cook soups and other things. This is an extremely healthy practice. Drinking purified water will help remove toxins from your body. Before you drink from a glass of water, hold it in your hands, and concentrate on this remarkable fluid. Doing so may enhance and energize its healing properties.

If you dream upon a pond of water, you might see fantastic inspirational visions which will inspire and enlighten you. Find the card **WATER LILY POND** in this deck, to see what I mean. Water is a symbol of purity and tranquility, and it is very calming to meditate on the ripples and waves in a pond or stream. Let us strive to keep the amazing water on our beautiful planet Earth as pure as we can, so that all life forms can benefit from its restorative and vitalizing properties. It is truly sacred to us all.

SANDMAN'S MAGIC
A special evening visitor

Who do you think visits you every night to give you dreams? It's the Sandman of course! He has a magical bag of sparkling sand that he sprinkles upon your eyes. You will then have amazing dreams of worlds beyond, visions of things that will be, and people from your long ago memories. You never know what type of magical images he will bring each evening, and amazing adventures he will transport you to. This mystical wizard has a host of little elves, fairies, and other spirit elementals who help him with his supernatural spells.

Prepare for your otherworldly visitor

Be ready for him when night comes, by tucking yourself in under the covers. Then think of what kind of dreams you would like to have. Perhaps you would enjoy visiting a realm of unbelievable fantasy that you've never experienced before. Or you might want to go to a place that you loved as a child, and want to visit again, with loved ones you haven't seen for years. Then paint a vividly colored "Mind Painting" of your upcoming dream in your imagination. Next, as you close your eyes, breathe deeply and slowly, as you relax your entire body. You will soon feel very comfortable and calm, as your sandman guardian approaches. You might then envision sparkling lights, twinkling and sparkling in the darkness. That is the Sandman's magic dust that he is putting upon your eyes from above! It is swirling all around your head, and making you feel cozy and very sleepy. Just go with his flow, and drift off to his enchanting world. It is a fascinating experience, as you well know. Before you fall asleep, you can try asking him to give you those special dreams that you were thinking about. He may do just that! He's really a very congenial and jolly fellow!

When morning comes, you will gradually unfold like a flower blooming in slow motion. Try to savor and remember the memories of the dreams you have had, before you jump out of bed. Just lie there for a few minutes, and review any lingering memories you may still have of your evening visions and adventures into Dreamland. Write them down if you can, and try to interpret their meanings. They can often be very helpful to you in your waking hours. Often, some of the first explanations that come to your mind might be the correct ones. You may know immediately what the symbols in your dreams mean, because they are very personal to you. It could be very enlightening if you keep a "dream journal," from which you can relive and remember them. Look forward to your sandman's magical visit each night.

SEASONS OF ENCHANTMENT
Enjoy all the seasons of life

All the world is amazing and wondrous, no matter who or where you are. Nature is in constant change and growth. To observe it all is an awesome experience.

Spring, Summer, Autumn, and Winter are all magnificent. When you consider how important they are, you will agree. Trees and flowers go through cycles of growth, fruition, and hibernation, until they bloom once again.

Animals and humans also have different stages of life, just as the trees and flowers. When we are young, we constantly develop and learn about the world, and this process continues throughout our lives, in its different stages. Fairies and other spiritual beings live in a world where they experience all of Life from a higher domain than our mortal world. They see all of the seasons at once, which is quite amazing. This painting shows how Fairies and their spirit guides, such as unicorns, overlook the change of seasons. All of nature is sacred to the world of fae, and they care for everything throughout the cycles of growth. Let us look at the awesome world through a fairy's eyes: See the beauty of the first tree buds of Spring begin to unfurl and become young leaves. Then feel the warm kisses of the Summer sun as it entices the lovely deeply-scented roses to bloom. The invigorating Autumn winds soon blow vividly colored leaves to earth. Afterwards, the crisp Winter cold creates gorgeous snowflakes to blanket the world as it sleeps, until the warm Spring air awakens nature to renew itself once again. Every season has its own unique spectacular beauty and meaning. The fairies watch over us and want us to cherish each season of life as something special, incomparable, and blessed.

Create something new

An idea for you to experience is to go "online" in your Mind, and create a very personal "Podcast" of the "Seasons of Life," all in your Imagination. When you finish it, you can remember and view it over and over again, whenever you desire. In your podcast, you can watch nature forms grow, as if you were watching time lapse photography. See a tiny seed develop to fruition, the sun rise and set, and flowers and trees change throughout the four seasons.

You can also make a "video" of your life growing and developing. Envision the seasons of your life, as you go through Spring, Summer, Autumn, and Winter. I'm sure your "Mind Podcast" will be very inspiring, enlightening, and exciting to see.

SHY VIOLET
Everyone goes through periods of feeling inadequate

Shyness is a very common thing that many people experience at some time in their lives. Not everyone shows it, but honestly, even famous people have moments of stage fright and shyness in front of others. I'm sure many have such feelings of inferiority at one time or another. But overcoming these difficult experiences can be empowering and strengthening.

The key is to have deep belief in yourself. Know your strengths and talents. When you see people who have had great achievements, most likely they have worked hard to gain their success. Don't feel badly that you have not attained great heights the way they have. Be inspired by these people, and seek to develop your own talents to the fullest, the way they have done. It's truly a wonderful experience to learn about the people you admire. Observe them closely, and study what they might have done to achieve greatness.

Imagining the "New You"

Sit in a quite room with your eyes closed, breathing slowly and deeply. Imagine looking into a secret mirror, where you see your image in a special way. Gaze deep into your very soul. There you will see your hidden talents appear within yourself, like flowers growing in slow motion. Many people know what abilities they have, and sometimes there are other gifts that we don't even know we possess. As you watch the blossoms of aptitudes within you growing to fruition, you will see ways to develop your own special genius. Sometimes it takes a lot of effort to realize your dreams. But it will be well worth the effort to do so. It will give you great joy to know that you've worked hard to become the best person you can be. But always be realistic, and be sure to understand your true abilities and fortes.

Meditation

Visualize a violet flower, remembering that this shy flower is very lovely, with the color of the crown chakra. Meditate on this sacred color and flower, which focuses on enlightenment, imagination, and peace within oneself. Violets are symbols of love, as you can see by their heart-shaped leaves.

These blossoms express honesty, dreams, and healing. This meditation will help you enjoy yourself to the fullest, and your own personal development in life.

52

SLEEPING BUNNY

Peaceful rest is essential to health

We all are in need of rest, in order to regenerate our souls and minds. Without the proper deep sleep and relaxation, we won't be able to function well in our daily lives. This could lead to serious health problems.

Take a lesson from our dear animal friends. We understand that they do lead active lives, but they know when it's time to eat and sleep. They live a simpler life than we do, and are very close to nature. And so we can learn many lessons from them. Observe animals closely and you will see that how very wise and natural they are.

Exercise

Pretend you are a soft warm and furry little bunny. You've had a long busy day running, hopping, visiting your little friends, and nibbling delicious food. Feeling very tired, you see the moon and stars, and know it's time to sleep. Yawn deeply by taking several slow motion deep breaths, and stretching your paws and arms wide. Then curl up in a comfortable position, one that you like the most. It could be on your back, or side, or stomach, whatever feels good to you. Cover yourself with a blanket or sheet if you like, as you close your eyes. As a human, you may have many unsolved thoughts and problems that have occupied you throughout the day. But this special time is to be a period of peaceful and restful sleep. So continue to breathe slowly and deeply, concentrating only on your breath rising and falling, in and out. At the same time, relax your entire body, concentrating on each part one at a time, from the feet up to your head. Make sure there is no stress in any of your muscles. If there is, relax them as best you can. Try not to think consciously of things. Let your mind go, and be aware only of your breathing, and relaxing your body. You might then see changing images and colors, slowly moving by, as if on a movie screen. While you are still aware of each deep breath, also watch your private movie that is playing in your mind. It will most likely be a "film" of transient images: some beautiful ones, and others very strange and surrealistic. You will probably drift off to sleep very soon. In the morning you will awaken feeling revived and refreshed. Pleasant dreams!

SWEET CREATURES
They will always cheer you

When we see sweet little animal pictures from our childhood memories, they always trigger a smile and happy thought. We had them as beloved stuffed toys that we cuddled, and they were our companions as we snuggled in our beds on the way to dreamland. Sometimes we even made little clothes for them, to dress them, and even invited them to share our parties, along with our other friends, both imaginary and real.

Today they may still be with us, even if only in our heartfelt memories.

And of course many of us have our cherished pets who live and love with us, and share our homes. They are our companions, friends, and dear family members. They give us unconditional love and we give them the same in return. We don't think of them as "just animals." To us, they are "human" friends too, and even our "fur babies" or "children," with feelings just like people have. To have dear loving pets, and to share kindnesses with them, is a true blessing.

Tell a story

Just for fun, why don't you try writing a little story about your beloved animal pet. This little friend may be with you now, or may no longer still be on our earth plane. They might be a little friend you had years ago, but who is still loved in your heart, and never forgotten, having gone over "the rainbow bridge." They could even be a little toy animal that you cherished. Whoever they are, writing a tender story about them would be a wonderful experience. You could imagine the things they do or did, and even make up some fantasy adventures that they could go on. This could be developed into a fascinating, and even healing experience for you. Talk to your little animal friend in real life, or in your imagination, and think of what they would say back to you. This dialogue could be part of your story. You might want to illustrate your animal tale, and even dress your little creature in adorable costumes, such as what Beatrix Potter did with her Peter Rabbit stories. It would be a real treat to see your story come alive, and your little animal friend will live forever in its pages. Enjoy this experience!

THOUGHTFULNESS
Keep your mind and abilities going strong

Our minds are such a precious gift to each of us. They keep us going throughout our lifetime, giving us wonderful ideas of creativity. We must keep our minds active and healthy. Some ways to do this are to be creative and alert. Be strong and self reliant, and don't become too dependent. Use your mind constantly. Do a puzzle, read a book, think about current events. Try to solve problems on your own. For instance if you lose something, try to reconstruct what you did before losing the object. Meditate on a difficult situation for a while, and plan the best way to resolve it, rather than making a rash decision which could get you into trouble later on.

If you enjoy the art of Literature, you might want to develop your talents as an author. Develop your skills of story telling, record thoughts in a personal diary, write letters to people, etc. Computers are a great aid to type or dictate your ideas into print. But don't let your hands become inactive and weak. The ability to do things with your hands is a wonderful talent to have. Try to transcribe some thoughts down on actual paper, with a pen, in cursive or printed words.

Exercise

Practice printing and writing a letter or posts into your personal diary. Write an original story or poem. And remember to take care of your hands. Don't overtax them so as to develop carpal tunnel syndrome. Take breaks when you are writing or typing on the computer. Do stretching exercises for your fingers and wrists. Moisturize your hands to keep the skin healthy, and keep your fingernails short so as to be able to keep them clean.

Have fun and try some "automatic writing," which is also called psychography. You might even start off with a pen and paper, just writing wriggling lines that aren't even recognizable as anything. As you look at the scribbles, they might resemble words, and you can just continue on in this way. At first, write what comes to mind, and don't even worry about whether or not it makes any sense. These thoughts might be coming from your unconscious mind. As you go along in this fashion, thoughts will coalesce in you head, and your ideas will become more clear. You might be surprised what pops out of your innate psychic abilities. If at first it still seems a bit confusing, enjoy analyzing and developing it more. This might evolve into a creative writing talent that you didn't even know you had! Enjoy the adventure of it all!

TOY BOX
Always keep your childhood memories safe within your heart

Remember your youth, no matter how recent it was, or how long ago. Childhood should never be something to be ashamed or made fun of. Our adult lives wouldn't be what they are today, if we hadn't passed through the road of childhood. It's a very healthy thing to sometimes think of our youthful days, both happy and sad. And remembering our dear family and friends of the past is also excellent. Even the experience of thinking about your favorite toys you played with when you were little, can be an extremely healing experience. Some lucky people have even saved a few cherished little things from those days gone by, such as a teddy bear, dolls, or a book. I feel that if you think about some of these keepsakes, and are able to actually touch them, that experience might bring a tear or two to your eyes. Joyful tears of remembrance are very healing. Let them flow out from your soul. Don't be afraid to cry.

We've all had high hopes and dreams when we were young. They might have been of what we wanted to be when we grew up, or fantastic images of amazing imaginary worlds. No matter what they might have been, you may still remember them. If you don't, never fear, they still lie kept hidden away safely in the deepest memories of your subconscious mind. It is very healing to access these beautiful feelings and visions that you had from years past.

Meditation

Close your eyes and imagine yourself young again. You can start by envisioning childhood memories, and see them change into other images which are secret and personal to you. They could be scenes from your childhood, fairy-tale stories, experiences you've had, or any number of other things. Try to remember dreams and aspirations from your youth of what you would like to become as an adult. If these aspirations didn't reach fulfillment, and you had to put them away for safekeeping, now is the time to uncover them. Plant the seeds of these dreams again in the garden of your mind, and watch them bloom to fruition. Let's see what your new vision looks like now. Create a "Mind Painting" in your imagination, of your dreams. When you open your eyes, write down your vision, or draw a picture of it. Create an actual "Mind Painting" of your aspirations on paper or canvas, in full color! You will be very proud to have discovered those dreams again.

TRANQUILITY
Find your sanctuary

A Pierrot sits by herself in an evening garden lit by the moon and stars. She finds some quiet time to be alone and think about her purpose in life and where she is going with it. Taking some "alone" time doesn't mean that you are lonely. We all require a secret space to meditate on our lives at times. We need to be with people too of course. To be able to compromise between being a social person, and having time alone for self reflection, is quite a healthy way of life.

Meditation

Find some special time when you can be alone without any distractions. It will be your secret retreat. Sit quietly in a chair with your eyes closed, and relax. Breathe slowly and deeply. Think about what road you are on in life, and what is your purpose. How do you feel about the relationships you have with people? What are the changes you would like to make in your life, if any? Are you happy in what you are doing?

I'm sure you have many personal questions you would like to ask of yourself. These are just a few to start. You will come up with many answers to think about. As you can see, quality time alone for self reflection is quite beneficial.

Look in the mirror

Another aspect which will be very helpful, is to improve yourself physically. Since you have some alone time now, you can be honest with yourself, and no one else will be privy to your self reflection. So look at yourself in a full length mirror. Study your image closely and honestly in every way that you can. Stand up tall and straight and try to be upright as much as you can. If you are a bit bent over, you will know you should work on developing better posture. Look closely and see if you are leaning slightly to one side more than another. Make sure your shoulders are at the same level and that your feet are pointing straight ahead. One way to help your upright stance is to lightly hold a strand of your hair on the top of your head, and extend it straight up, pulling it very gently. It will make you feel as if there is a cord attached to your head, pulling you up so that you can stand perfectly erect. Practice walking around the room with your head held high. See how else you can improve yourself. It might also be helpful to take exercise classes, or physical therapy. Do some research on which path to take.

TWILIGHT MEAL

The wholesome ways of nature

We should love and respect all of nature: The trees and other plants, the air we breath, and the water we drink. They are all sacred to us, without which we could not survive. So we should strive as best we can to keep our planet pure and free from pollution.

Animals play a very important part in the life of this planet also. These precious creatures enjoy life in every way. They can fly and run, leap and soar. How amazing they are! You can learn many lessons from them if you take time to observe these blessed beings closely. They are our brothers and sisters on this beautiful planet Earth, and we should nurture and respect them and all other life forms on it, as well as humankind of course.

Let's snuggle up alongside these two adorable little wild rabbits in my painting, and see what they're up to, as they eat their twilight evening meal of clover.

Diet tips from the animals

When you watch an animal eat, you will see that they chew their food <u>extremely well</u> before they swallow it. Please remember that it's not just <u>what</u> you eat, it's also <u>how</u> you eat it! Try eating smaller portions, chewing your food slowly and well, and putting just a little bit on your fork or spoon at a time. It tastes more delicious that way too. You will feel satisfied quicker, and so you will eat a bit less. Some people gulp and "drink" their food down very quickly. As a result, they may get indigestion, and still want more and more, never being quite satisfied because it's not chewed up well.

Animals in the wild eat lots of fresh greens, leaves, fruits, nuts, and seeds of all kinds. That could serve as a clue to us—to eat as naturally as we can. Try to find organically grown GMO-free foods in the store, without sprays of harsh chemical insecticides. They will be healthier for you. Take some natural healthy supplements each day, and drink plenty of good water. Try to cut down on using salt, sugar, and caffeine. And add healthy things to your meals such a fresh fruits and vegetables. You will feel better eating the more natural way like our dear animal friends.

WATER LILY POND
Never stop dreaming

To daydream is a wonderful experience. It sets the mind free to wander and contemplate imaginative thoughts. Fascinating ideas could develop from dreaming on clouds, water, a flower, or anything else that you might enjoy dreaming upon. It is like scrying into a crystal ball, and seeing messages come forth. They could be messages from your spirit or animal guides, angel guardians, or from deep inside your mind and soul.

Meditation

I invite you to step into my painting of a young boy gazing into a waterlily pond with goldfish. Sit alongside him and join in his reverie. See what comes to mind as you watch the goldfish gracefully swim through the water, and observe the ripples that they make. What visions appear to you in the pond? Try this meditation at various times, in different ways if you like. You most certainly will see some imaginative pictures from your unconscious mind, of other worlds. Remember them. Jot down any interesting ideas which came to you during this meditation. Write a story about them, or create a diary of your creative thoughts.

Do an Automatic Drawing

Drawing pictures of the images that you saw would certainly be a delightful outlet for your imagination. Try another "Automatic Drawing," or "Mind Drawing," similar to what I described in my card "OUR ANIMAL FRIENDS." These images may express your own subconscious mind, such as dreams and images that you've kept inside for a long time and have forgotten. These "visions" could be of magnificent celestial planes above our own, or apparitions of the future that well up from your inner self. Whatever appears in your imagination will certainly be fascinating. Try doing a soft "scribble" or "doodle" with a pencil on paper. Don't draw it too dark at first, because you can more easily correct and change it if the lines are light. Keep a "kneaded" eraser handy. Think of what it looks like to you, and then develop it more into a finished drawing or painting. When you finally know that your drawing is the way you want it to be, you can add some darker sections. The Surrealist artists have often used similar techniques to create their fantastical artwork. It can be very enlightening to see your unconscious "Mind Painting" creations become realities. You might learn some new intriguing things about yourself.

WINTER DELIGHT

There is warmth even in the icy cold

This cheerful wide-eyed Holly Fairy loves the festive Wintertime. Even though the temperatures may be freezing, and the air nippy, it doesn't bother her a bit. She is the most happy when sparkling snowflakes fall. A big smile appears on her cheerful red-cheeked face and she giggles with glee when snowflakes tickle her nose. The blanket of snow creates a magical world covering her enchanted realm.

She is dressed in the bright ***red color*** of her holly berries. This color is the first root chakra, with positive attributes of courage, excitement, survival, a sense of security, and energy. Oh to be like the cheerful little Holly Fairy! She makes a seemingly difficult environment into a world of playfulness and magic. You can imagine being like her in the following exercise.

Daydream

Picture yourself as this pretty fairy, sitting jauntily on her berry bush, smiling joyfully. The air is cold, the snow is falling, but she hasn't a care in the world. Little Holly loves her world! It's a perfect place for her. Envision yourself doing what she loves to do: dance and twirl in the air with the snowflakes, lie on a blanket of snow, and sled down the hills with the other snow elves and fairies. She's never cold, or at a loss to have fun, and always enjoys the winter season. So enjoy every season of your life: Spring, Summer, Autumn, and Winter. They all have a delightful beauty of their own.

Other REDFeather Titles by the Author:
Inspirational Visions Oracle Cards, ISBN 978-0-7643-6000-8

Other REDFeather Titles on Related Subjects:
Magical Dimensions Oracle Cards and Activators, 2nd edition, Lightstar, ISBN 978-0-7643-6435-8

The Twilight Realm: A Tarot of Faery, Beth Wilder, ISBN 978-0-7643-3393-4

Higher Intuitions Oracle, Kristy Robinett and Johna Gibson Bowman, ISBN 978-0-7643-4143-4

Copyright © 2022 by Judy Mastrangelo

Library of Congress Control Number: 2022932791

All rights reserved. No part of this work may be reproduced or used in any form or by any means—graphic, electronic, or mechanical, including photocopying or information storage and retrieval systems—without written permission from the publisher.

The scanning, uploading, and distribution of this book or any part thereof via the Internet or any other means without the permission of the publisher is illegal and punishable by law. Please purchase only authorized editions and do not participate in or encourage the electronic piracy of copyrighted materials.

"Red Feather Mind Body Spirit" logo is a trademark of Schiffer Publishing, Ltd.
"Red Feather Mind Body Spirit Feather" logo is a registered trademark of Schiffer Publishing, Ltd.

Designed by Jack Chappell
Cover design by Danielle Farmer
Type set in Romance Fatal/Minion

ISBN: 978-0-7643-6532-4
Printed in China

Published by REDFeather Mind, Body, Spirit
An imprint of Schiffer Publishing, Ltd.
4880 Lower Valley Road
Atglen, PA 19310
Phone: (610) 593-1777; Fax: (610) 593-2002
Email: Info@redfeathermbs.com
Web: www.redfeathermbs.com

For our complete selection of fine books on this and related subjects, please visit our website at www.redfeathermbs.com. You may also write for a free catalog.
REDFeather Mind, Body, Spirit's titles are available at special discounts for bulk purchases for sales promotions or premiums. Special editions, including personalized covers, corporate imprints, and excerpts, can be created in large quantities for special needs. For more information, contact the publisher.
We are always looking for people to write books on new and related subjects. If you have an idea for a book, please contact us at proposals@schifferbooks.com.